CW00376466

Understand
From Your Own Limitations

MATTHEW BRIGHTHOUSE

Table of Contents

Introduction

You have taken the Myers-Briggs personality test and you have discovered your personality type. Now, you might be wondering exactly what those four letters mean, so let's take a look.

Finding out about your personality is a wonderful thing to do because it allows you to understand yourself much better, develop your strengths, understand and develop your weaknesses, whilst allowing you the chance to understand other people better too. We all have strengths, which make us a force to be reckoned with in various different situations, but as human beings, we all have weaknesses too. Understanding these weaknesses is key to effective personal development.

It's vital to know that weaknesses do not in effect make us weak, they make us human and they are part of who we are. They are not a huge negative. What you can do, however, is learn from those weaknesses, and stop them from potentially putting roadblocks in the way of opportunities in your life. Learning about these different personality types also allows you to understand why people act the way they do and react to situations. It's a great idea to learn about all of the personality types in the spectrum, especially if you are going to move into the business world; as an ESTP, you're perfectly placed to do just that! Effective people management relies on the ability to be able to understand people and why they do what they do. If you can understand this, you really have the key to being able to manage and develop your staff to the best of their ability and beyond.

Back to You ...

So, you have found yourself to be an ESTP personality type. You are someone full of life, you are a leader, a character, and you are hugely sociable. You do not like to live life in constraints, and you have no time for rules – you are a rule breaker in many ways! You are known as The Entrepreneur, and you make up just 4% of the general population. You're rare, and that makes you special!

The ESTP personality type is a fascinating one to learn about because there are two very different sides to this character. On the one hand, you are someone who is logical, intelligent and measured in your actions, but on the other side, you're someone who is very prone to spontaneous and risky decision making, and you don't hold back, you tell it exactly how it is! There is a lot of room to work within this personality type, and that means you can develop yourself to huge levels, to allow you to really shoot for the stars, in whatever endeavor you put your mind to.

Before we continue, it's important to point out that nothing in this book is intended to offend or upset. Weaknesses are not there to be lectured about, they are there because they are part of who you are. Every single personality type has them, you're not alone! As a human being, we have strengths and we have weaknesses, this is what makes us feel and be alive; if we didn't have them, life would be rather boring. The point is to ensure that your weaknesses aren't putting obstacles in the way of progress and success.

So, without further ado, let's start our journey into the thrilling and exciting world of the ESTP personality type, and learn more about what makes you tick!

1

The Fine Line Between Strength And Weakness

Your personality test told you that you are an ESTP personality type. Now you know those important four letters, you can begin learning more about yourself at your very core. First things first though, what exactly does the Myers-Briggs tell you?

Basically, by answering the questions and identifying yourself as an ESTP, you now have the tools to learn more about what makes you tick. You can understand why you react the way you do to yourself situations in your life, and you can also put into place mechanisms that can help you take advantage of situations and opportunities, rather than perhaps repeating old patterns that have not served you well in the past. You will now be able to learn about those strengths and weaknesses we talked about in our introduction section, and you will be able to develop those in either direction, depending on what they are and what they mean to you.

Next up, we need to know what those four letters actually mean.

E = Extroversion
S = Sensing
T = Thinking
P = Perception

You still probably don't have the first clue what that all means in terms of your personality, so let's explore it a little more.

Extroversion

You are an outgoing soul, someone who is a born leader and the life and soul of the party. You are not a wallflower, and you are not someone who observes and thinks, rather than speaking. ESTPs make great team leaders and managers, because of those fantastic leadership qualities, and they have an inspirational side, which pushes other people around them to go out of their own comfort zones and reach their own potential.

The downside of this particular trait is that, alongside some other traits, you have the tendency to be a little insensitive from time to time. This is something we're going to talk about in more detail throughout the book, to help you minimize this becoming an issue for you.

Sensing

Working alongside perception, which we will talk about shortly, you are someone who can think very deeply about an issue and come up with a logical and creative solution. You think fast, and you think on your feet. Whilst forward planning might not be your forte, when you are in the heat of the moment, you have the gift of being able to understand what is going on, and you can quickly come up with an answer to whatever is in front of you. Again, this works wonderfully well with your entrepreneurial and management skills, avoiding any disasters before they happen.

Thinking

You are logical and creative at the same time, which is a fantastic mixture! You are very perceptive to change and you can roll and adapt very easily. You are not someone who fears change and what it brings, you are someone who embraces it and moves to allow it to occur. You base your decisions on evidence and that allows you to make good decisions, most of the time. The danger for the ESTP personality type, however, is that when you become bored, you may have the tendency to make spontaneous and rash decisions, that could lead you to hot water if you're not careful. Learning to think for a few seconds before acting, is enough to iron this potential issue out.

Perception

One of the key strengths as an ESTP is your highly tuned perception levels. You can notice a change in someone very quickly, even by just a nod of the head, or a roll of the eyes. You are able to understand someone's motives with your perception and intelligence, and this is a very positive trait to have. You are also able to understand if someone is a little 'off' for some reason, by their actions and their words. When you can learn to use this perceptive gift for positives in your life, you can really go far.

Now we know what those four letters mean, you will be able to start putting the skeleton of your personality type together in your head. There are many gaps to fill in at this point, but you can see by now that you are someone who is outgoing, a leader, someone who is perceptive and astute, and someone who is always on the lookout for the next adventure to go on. So, to further fill in those gaps, let's explore your ESTP strengths and weaknesses.

ESTP Strengths

First, in the interest of positivity, let's explore the wonderful and plentiful strengths you have as part of your ESTP personality type.

Full of Life
You are brimming with life and you have a true lust for whatever you set your mind to. You don't bother with anything which bores you, and that means that you can really focus on the projects that bring you joy. Of course, when you do this, you do a better job, so it works both ways for you. You are bold, you go forth and conquer, sidestepping any obstacle in your way with ease. You think on your feet, and you think fast. This trait is what attracts many people towards you, both romantically and in terms of being an inspiration and a role model. It's no wonder that so many people with ESTP personality types go on to be real entrepreneurs in their trade, because of this fearless streak which means they conquer whatever is in front of them.

Quite Practical
Despite the fact that you do have a reckless streak within your personality, and we'll talk in much more detail about that later, you are also able to be quite practical and also quite rational when thinking and making decisions. You don't make these decisions beforehand because you're not a planner, but when you're forced to make them in the heat of the moment, you quickly scan all the information you

have to hand and you make a rational and very practical decision based on what is in front of you. This ability is another reason why you are likely to succeed in business endeavors, because when something comes up unexpectedly, you can make the right choice, to steer the business in the most successful of directions.

Totally Unique
You are an original and anyone who tries to copy you will be a very poor copy indeed! You come up with original ideas, original styles, and everything you do is totally unique to you. This means that you're likely to be a pioneer, someone who moves forward through life fearlessly, with a 'what will be, will be' attitude. Again, this is a very inspirational to many people around you, and also makes you a fantastic team leader. The ability to inspire and lead people with a unique approach and a bold attitude is something which guarantees success on many different levels.

Very Perceptive
We have touched upon this already when describing your personality type, but you re hugely perceptive. The ability to be able to see what is going on beneath the surface, simply by observing a quirk of the eyebrow, or a roll of the eyes, is something that comes very naturally to you. This means you can pick up on changes or motives very easily, and avoid disaster. The downside is that you also have the tendency to call people out of these motives without really thinking of the consequences! Again, this is something we'll talk about in more detail later, but for now, just know that your perceptive ability is beyond

measure, and you can use that in many different avenues of your life.

No Mind Games

You are extremely direct, you say it how it is, and you tell it as you want to. You are direct, and that means that people around you know where they stand, with no grey areas at all. Of course, this could be a downside too, because your delivery of 'how it is' is sometimes a little on the overly direct side, but being a very straight down the line person has some major advantages, especially in business. Everyone around you knows exactly where they stand, and nobody is confused or asking endless questions.

The Life And Soul of The Party

You are a true social butterfly! Whilst you won't waste time on functions that don't interest you, when you do attend a gathering of some kind, you're likely to be in the middle of it! People are drawn to you like a magnet, and that is why you are such a great leader. Your charisma and your 'this is how it is' attitude to life are inspiring to so many people around you, and that means that when you talk, people listen.

ESTP Weaknesses

We all have them! The idea of explaining your weaknesses is so that you can work on them and minimize the effect they have on your life. This isn't meant to change you at your very core, quite the opposite! The idea is to develop, not to change completely.

So, what are the main ESTP weaknesses?

A Tendency Towards Insensitivity

You don't really deal with emotions, and you don't acknowledge your own that much. This means that when you speak, or when you call someone out on their motives, you have a tendency towards being a little insensitive. Of course, you don't mean this to hurt someone, it's genuinely that you just aren't as emotional as others at your very core, and that you are more straight down the line, this is how it is. We mentioned that you don't play mind games, and you don't beat around the bush when you're speaking either. The problem is, when you're dealing with someone who is more emotionally charged than you, there can be conflict or even upset. Learning to curb this just a little, and perhaps become a little more in touch with your own emotions, will give you the power to sidestep these potential issues, and also lead you towards further power in being in touch with your own feelings.

An Impatient Nature

You don't like waiting for anything, and whatever it is you're wanting, you want it right now! This impatience can lead you towards taking shortcuts in situations that lead you down incorrect roads. If you'd just waited, been a little more patient, then what you were waiting for probably would have manifested anyway, but in its own time. Learning to wait, take a few minutes, and don't be in such a rush to get through life, will serve you well!

A Risky Streak

You have a streak within your personality that calls out for adventure and risk on a regular basis. Whilst this is great in some ways, because life should be lived with passion and adventure, it can sometimes lead you towards some risky situations. We're going to talk later in the book about how it's important to balance risk versus gain, and how there are good risks in life, and bad ones. Taking the good risks is always to be encouraged, but those bad risks should be weighed up and sidestepped if at all possible. If you can learn to do this, by taking a second to look before you leap, then you will be able to maximize the effects of your good risk-taking endeavors and minimize the negative risks.

Don't Have Time For Rules

You aren't someone who loves to live by rules, and you don't flourish well in structured environments. For instance, if you work within an office, on a 9-5 basis, within four walls, you're likely to feel trapped and suffocated. At school, it's likely that you felt like you wanted to break free. ESTPs can't be contained, they want to be free, and they want to explore, making decisions on the fly and going for whatever is in their hearts and minds. Whilst this is a positive in so many ways, it's important to realize that sometimes in life we have to go by the rules and that rules are there for a reason, usually our own safety. You are often defiant in the face of such structure, but earning to take a breath, count to ten, and understand the reasons behind it, will serve you well. It is also another reason why entrepreneur characteristics tend to lie within ESTP's. Having the freedom to roam and create your own visions.

A Tendency to Overlook The Bigger Picture

When rushing to get from one place to another, making decisions as you go, and trouble solving on the fly, you might miss out on the bigger picture. You live for today, and you don't like to make plans or think about the future, because what will be, will be. That's true, and in many ways that is a good, stress-free way to live, but in order to get to where we really want to go, e.g. achieving our dreams and fulfilling our potential, we need to make plans from time to time. By acknowledging the bigger picture in life, we can truly go far.

So there you have it, the upsides and downsides of being an ESTP. We've talked about the good and we've talked about the not so good, and now we're going to show you how to maximize those good points, and minimize those negative points.

2

Learn to Look Before You Leap

As an ESTP, you are someone who lives for today, you are someone who pushes boundaries in order to find out the truth, to have a good time, and also to see where roads take you. You are not someone who plans and thinks about things ten times over before doing them, before deciding not to do them at all. If you encounter a problem, you fix it along the way, using your logic and your creative mind to come up with solutions that get you around any obstacle.

There are some serious positives in living for the day. For a start, you have an idea and you go for it, you don't procrastinate, and you don't ever have to wonder 'what if'. People love that you just cast your cares aside and throw yourself into any idea you have a passion for. Many people look upon your vigor quite admirably, and rightly so! You never have to wonder what would happen if you'd only been brave enough to go for it, because you did it and you found out for yourself. You probably also managed to side-step anything which got in your way.

The thing is, nobody can ride their luck for that long, before a roadblock turns into a major quarry and you end up going over the handlebars of your bicycle, so to speak. Whilst we would never want to calm down that vigor for life and that bravery, it's important to do some thinking beforehand, in order to identify whether a situation is risky or not. A little risk is fine, even a moderate amount of risk is okay if you weigh up the pros and cons, but a large amount of risk is never a good road to go down.

As an ESTP, your 'live for today' attitude can sometimes land you in hot water, because you don't always think about the consequences. Having that 'I'll sort it out if, and when, it happens' attitude works most of the time, and admirably so, but not all the time. When it doesn't work, the consequences have the potential be catastrophic and dire.

Because we need to weigh up risk versus benefit in life, it's a good idea to try and think about the amount of risk involved before you leap. We're not saying you have to draw a flowchart of the potential outcomes of a situation before you go for it here, because that would go totally against the feel of your personality type anyway, but if something really is risky, and if it could end up taking you down a dark road, do give it more thought than you would normally.

You're probably used to friends and relatives telling you that 'you're crazy' to do whatever it is you're considering doing, and you're right to not pay that much attention to this always. Many people put the 'you're crazy' tag on someone who has the bravery to do something that they wish they had the bravery to do, but sometimes they're being literal. Sometimes that idea isn't a good one, and sometimes they're only telling you their take on it because they care and they're worried about your health and wellbeing.

A good way to think about this is to question whether you'd be happy if your son or daughter was about to do what you're thinking of doing. Would you tell them they were crazy? Or, would you say 'great, go for it?' It's good to think this way because you would never allow your child to do something that would put them in harm, whether you had your ESTP reckless head on or not.

Can you see where we're going with this? Switching your view and seeing it from the outside in, from the perspective of someone with true love and concern at the heart of it all, will allow you to assess whether your actions are the good type of risky, or the bad type of risky.

What is 'Look Before You Leap'?

Look before you leap can really be used to explain several different situations. But in terms of the ESTP personality type and its general traits, we're using it to explain the fact that your personality type is prone to making risky decisions, because tomorrow is another day. You hate to be put in a box and constrained, and a lot of your risky decisions are down to that. You're much more likely to make a poor choice if you're feeling boxed in. The best way to avoid that is, to try and avoid feeling boxed in in the first place! Of course, that's not easy, but changing your mindset is the best place to start.

Work isn't something to box you in, if you're not happy with your job, you can change it. This is a good type of risky. If you're not feeling happy in a relationship and you're genuinely feeling too tied down and unhappy, it's time to have a conversation and assess whether you should stay in that partnership. These are types of situations that could leave you feeling boxed in, which you can avoid. If you can avoid that, then you are going to avoid making decisions that are dangerous or risky, and therefore avoid the possibility of harm.

Now, we're certainly not suggesting that as an ESTP you're reckless to the extreme, and that you don't think at all, because you are actually very intelligent, it's just that your drive for a thrill and your need to be free can often cloud your judgment. This isn't all of the time either. It may be useful to keep a journal of the way you're feeling and see if you can spot a pattern. If you're feeling like you want to head off and do something crazy, perhaps throw away your job and go traveling without any savings, just as an example, see if you can spot a reason for why that is. Are you going through a period of stress? Is it someone at work that is causing you to want to leave? What is the reason? Fixing the reason will help you avoid a poor decision that could potentially lead you down the wrong road.

Of course, if you simply want to be spontaneous and head off for the day, do something crazy like sit under the stars for no reason, that's a good kind of impulsive, and we're all for those spontaneous and good adventures!

3

Learn to Harness Your Energy And Perceptiveness For Positives

As an ESTP, you would make a great private investigator. You can spot a change in someone from a mile away, and you don't even have to know them that well. A simple raise of an eyebrow at the wrong moment and you can suss out someone's motives easily.

You have a highly tuned sense of perception that is useful when trying to understand someone's real intentions in a situation. Not many people can claim to have that gift, and a lot of people can tie themselves up in knots trying to figure out a situation out. You don't have that problem, and you have a boundless amount of energy to go alongside it. You're a seeker of the truth!

It's vital to be able to use that gift for good. This book isn't all about pointing out the weaknesses of an ESTP and telling you how not to do things that way, it's about taking down walls and avoiding barriers to success. Yes, some of your weaknesses create situations and limitations in life that you need to try and avoid, but that is the same for every personality type. It's also about celebrating your strengths and learning to develop them to higher levels, to harness their power for good. In your case, this particular gift is something you can really push on and develop.

The downside of perception, when combined with the ESTP no-nonsense attitude, is that if you do notice something 'off' about a person or a situation, you have the tendency to call them out on it there and then, without much sensitivity going into it! This can get you into trouble, because although most of the time you're not wrong, there is a way of going about speaking to someone, and you sometimes don't opt for the right road. If you can learn to take a step back before approaching the person and questioning them on what is happening, then you will find that the negative situation doesn't happen as often.

There are certain types of job which you would be ideal for, aside from the private investigator idea. At work, you are often gifted at understanding how a deal is going to go because you can read body language and shifts in attitude. For this reason, business dealings are your thing – you 're not called the entrepreneur for anything! You have that creative problem-solving mind, with a large dollop of logic, and that can allow you to get around any potential business-related pitfalls, with a large amount of creative thinking. The ability to read people serves you well in these situations. In addition, you would also make a very good policeman or policewoman. Again, if you can harness the desire to want to jump straight in both feet, without thinking things through, then you would be ideal at understanding motives and the real story behind the mask.

On a personal level, however, understanding a shift or change in someone's feelings or attitudes can also be used for good too. Whilst you're not the most sensitive of people, and you find it hard to communicate on an 'I feel ...' level, if you can get in touch with your emotions just a little (more on that later), then you can understand the real story behind a person's behavior. For instance, if a loved one has become withdrawn or quiet, and they are quite snappy with everyone around them, it could be tempting to just withdraw and let them get on with it, but if you use your perception to understand that there is indeed a problem, you could be the one to save them from silence. Not everyone has the ability to be able to see what is going on beneath the surface, but you do.

A Boundless Energy

On top of your highly tuned perception, you are also someone who has a huge amount of energy – when it is related to something you feel passionate about. If you can find causes that really call out to your core feelings and beliefs, you're likely to move mountains to make them successful. Again, you'll conquer any problem that you come up against, because that's what ESTPs do!

In order to use this strength of yours for the greater good, it's important to choose your battles wisely. You will lose interest if you're not fully invested in a project, so make sure you pick out your projects with a little careful thinking. Yes, this is going to mean that you need to adopt the limitation we talked about in our last chapter, e.g. learning to look before you leap a little, but you will find the benefits and rewards are great if you can do this.

Overall, using your perception and strength for the greater good is all down to toning down your need to jump in with both feet and confront the issue, and to try and adopt a little more sensitivity. If you can do this, there really will be no stopping you.

4

Learn How to Acknowledge And Express Your Emotions

Moving on from our last chapter, this particular issue links in really well. Basically, as an ESTP you have difficulty in not only understanding the emotional side of people, but also expressing your deepest feelings too. This isn't something you should feel negative about because there are a huge number of people out there who don't find it easy to talk about how they feel too. However, if you can side-step or jump over this hurdle, you will find that life suddenly becomes a lot easier on many levels.

Later on, in our book, we're going to talk about relationships and the ESTP personality type. As an ESTP, you're a very fun loving person, and you're someone who people don't get bored around. You're also someone who is easily bored, and someone who flits from idea to idea without really finishing anything, unless you feel totally committed and invested. The same can be said for your relationships. You find it hard to express the way you feel, so instead of addressing it and communicating with your partner, you may decide to leave beforehand. This isn't just about relationships, it can be about any type of emotional situation in your life. You may not feel that comfortable with your feelings and expressing them.

Now, how can you change that? And, why should you change that? You've got this far in life, why do you need to suddenly start telling people how you feel now? Well basically, if you can be more in tune with your emotions, you will be more intuitive, your relationships will improve, your friendships will improve, your stress levels will be reduced, and you'll basically feel a lot more at ease within yourself. You'll also be able to handle situations with other people much more sensitively too, without potentially upsetting someone and not being aware of it. If you don't 'do' feelings, then when you deal with someone who is more emotionally charged than you, the situation can become difficult on both sides.

Learning to understand your emotions is about accepting them first. Acknowledging your feelings can be difficult, especially if it leads to unearthing difficult emotions, but it's important to deal with this and move on. The first step to being more emotionally aware of yourself and others is in acknowledgment.

So, try this exercise for a couple of weeks and see how you feel at the end of it. Keep a journal, and at the end of every day write down the way you feel. Did you feel angry that day about anything? Identify the reason and the way it made you feel inside. Did you feel happy? Why and how did that feel? Did you come into contact with someone who was upset, happy, angry, joyful, jealous? Try and identify why (if you can), and how coming into contact with that emotion made you feel too.

At the end of the two weeks journal keeping, you will see that it's not that you don't have emotions, of course you do, it's just that it is your personality to keep them buried or to simply brush them under the carpet. Your personality type doesn't place a huge amount of importance on feelings, and that's fine, but if you want to knock down limitations in your personality type, then this is one of the biggest hurdles to get over. This journal will help you see that you feel a million emotions in the space of a day, and whilst most of them don't mean anything, some do. It's important to acknowledge the ones that are important, and to act on the reasons and triggers for them, for good or bad. This exercise will help you become more aware of the way you feel, and that is a huge positive.

Of course, once you start doing this, you will also begin to be more aware of the feelings of others too. By doing this, you can start to tailor your communication style when dealing with a person who you can see is more openly emotional. Even people who aren't openly demonstrative about the way they feel have feelings, and you will also be able to be generally more sympathetic and sensitive overall. This is a part of your personality that you can open up and work on over time, and it is a part which will allow you to really work hand in hand with that gift of perception we were talking about in our last chapter.

Again, by knocking down this limitation and moving it out of your way, you will clear the road for greater opportunities.

5
Learn How to Avoid Missing The Bigger Picture

What exactly is the 'bigger picture' you might be asking? Is it the distant future? Is it the reasons behind a certain situation? It's really a little of both.

As an ESTP, one of your weaknesses is, as we have mentioned, a tendency to look before you leap and sometimes land yourself in hot water. We've already addressed a couple of ways to try and curb that tendency away from risky decisions and more towards the good side of risky, but how do you avoid missing that bigger picture in life?

All of these traits are linked, as you will be able to see, and this particular limitation is about a lack of future planning. You are not someone who likes plans and itineraries drawn up; you do not like to be put in a box and harnessed, you like to be free; you *need* to be free! Deep down, you fear that thinking about the future and making plans is going to tie you down to the point where you're not able to be spontaneous and just go for things that make you happy.

This isn't the case in reality.

Plans aren't there to be rigid, they are more like guidelines. We all need to plan a little in life, otherwise we'd just bumble from one situation to another, and never really reach the dreams and aims we hold dear. For instance, if you want to build your own business empire, how are you supposed to achieve that if you don't put in place a plan to get you there? The clouds are not going to rain down a huge business opportunity that suddenly lands in your lap; you need to plan, work at it, invest, make mistakes, learn from them, and grow. This is how you achieve what you want in life and reach your potential. A lack of planning doesn't make this happen, and if it does, it's a huge fluke of luck.

You are someone who goes for something they feel strongly about, and if a problem occurs, you creatively get over it, usually succeeding. Now, that's great, but what about those situations that a little planning could have helped you with? How do you know you're not missing something major? This is what we mean by the bigger picture.

Thinking carefully and making plans will help you see the bigger picture. And by doing that, you can put into place a few ideas that can get you there much faster and more successfully. We're not suggesting you write down an itinerary and stick to it like glue, but a few rough outlines on a suggested route it all it takes. The danger of not doing this is that you totally miss it, and you end up moving from one idea to the next, never really succeeding completely. If you miss the bigger picture, you miss your potential. Dear ESTP, as this entrepreneurial, highly energetic and perceptive personality type, you have a wealth of potential that is untapped, and if you can figure out how to open that Pandora's Box, you will be someone who will be a true force to be reckoned with.

One very famous ESTP personality type is Madonna.

Now, Madonna is not someone who plays by the rules, she is not someone who conforms to the general guidelines, but she is a businesswoman at heart; this is how she has become the huge multi-million dollar empire she is, and how she has turned the face of music and modern pop culture on its head. Do you think Madonna managed to do all of this without planning and thinking carefully? No. Whilst her talent and a little luck probably worked for her some of the way, her shrewd business mind was what really pushed her far.

You can be like Madonna, in whatever field you choose, but the ability to plan and understand that this isn't a form of boxing you in is vital.

6

Learn How to Harness Your Vigor For Life And Tenacity in Business Endeavors

Oh, that boundless energy! We have talked already about your highly tuned perception and your great energy levels, but how can you use those, especially your energy, to help you in your business endeavors?

We have also mentioned that you are known as 'The Entrepreneur', so that suggests that at your core, you have a very good business mind. This is true, but as an ESTP you need to have a passion for whatever it is you're creating, in order to see it through. If you're not invested fully, you will simply become frustrated, throw in the towel, and move on to something else.

So, how can you use your energy and lust for life, to make your business idea work?

Firstly, it's about choosing an idea that really gets you excited. We talked in our first 'learn to ...' chapter about how you can try and learn to look before leaping, because otherwise, you can make risky decisions. This is where thinking about what really gets your juices flowing can help you, because if you look before you leap into something that is positive and doesn't have any downsides, then there is no real risk involved!

So, sit down and think, what makes you excited? What area of business would you really feel passionate about, to the point where that passion would only grow, and wouldn't become boring? Try and avoid the temptation to jump towards the first idea you come up with here, and think it through a few times. Once you have an idea, that is your good type of risky!

Once you have that exciting idea, it's time to do a little planning. Again, we mentioned this in our last chapter, but part of minimizing risk but maximizing success is about the ability to think and plan a little. Remember our Madonna comparison? This is where that really comes to truth. Brainstorm, keep the excitement within you, come up with ideas and suggestions, and talk to someone you trust about it, to get their ideas and input too.

If you find that your energy is waning and you don't feel as piqued by the idea, then you know it's not the right one, but if your idea is making you feel excited, then keep on with it, and don't give up.

This boundless energy is something you can harness in the right direction, and if you can do that, it will push you to greatness. Your problem-solving talent, thinking on your feet, is perfect in the business world, but it is important to minimize risk by making well thought out decisions, not ones you jumped into with your eyes closed. It's about grabbing those positive traits and trying to minimize the effects of the negative ones.

Your ESTP passion and energy will certainly be something that will help you get on board with prospective investors and business partners. Your personality type, when excited, speaks in a very passionate and enticing way, and you can charm the socks off anyone. Use this to your advantage! Harness that energy and direct it in the right direction.

7
Learn How to be a More Committed Partner

A relationship with an ESTP is never going to be dull or boring. Every single day there will be some new venture around, or an adventure to go on. This is great, but how great depends on the type of person you are with.

For instance, if you are with someone who is more grounded, someone who is emotionally-led and craves home security, then they are not going to cope too well with your spontaneous nature, and your occasional lack of sensitivity. Of course, we have explored that this is because you are less emotionally charged and less in touch with your emotions than some other people are, and this is something we have encouraged you to work on in an earlier chapter.

ESTP's do not tend to plan and like to live in the moment, as we have explored already. Whilst this has man upsides, the downside comes when we are talking about relationships. Unless you are in a relationship with someone who is equally as 'live for today', then they may find your lack of commitment to the future frustrating. Some people need a reassurance that the relationship is going somewhere, especially if the union has been for a considerable amount of time already.

It's not that the ESTP personality type is opposed to marriage, long relationships, or unions, it is that they simply don't like to be tied down to a future plan, with no wriggle room. When this happens, there is the tendency to want to break out and do something reckless, as we mentioned in our first 'learn to ...' chapter. The key to this? Communication.

As with any relationship, talking about how you feel is vital. Whilst you're not so in touch with your emotions, not yet anyway, unless you can open up a little and manage to get over to the other person how you do feel, the relationship may be doomed. You don't have to make sweeping, grand gestures of love, and you don't have to pour your heart out either; simply explaining in the plainest terms possible about how you feel is enough. "I do see my future with you, but for now let's just go with the flow". That tells the other person how you feel and reassures them. Of course, it may not be enough for some people who are more focused on security, and in that case, you may be pushed for more answers. Avoid the temptation to burst into anger or run away, take a deep breath and count to ten.

The problem is, for some people the explanation of 'I just don't want to feel tied down' can be misunderstood. That is the literal feeling you have, that you just don't live your life in a box, but it can be read as you saying that you want to keep your options open. Can you see the problem?

Basically, if this relationship is important to you, then you have to work on opening up and seeing a future with some plans for it. Jumping from relationship to relationship is fun for so long, usually when you're a little younger, but there may come a time when you want to settle down. Don't allow your desire to live in the here and now to take away your future security and happiness. Open up and make those tentative plans. Of course, if the other person is rushing you and wanting to set a full on itinerary of life, you're well within your rights to put on the brakes and say "slow down, you're making me uncomfortable", but a few tentative ideas about where your relationship may go is totally harmless. Don't see it as being 'trapped', see it as the wonderful thing that it is – someone loves you enough to want to make a life with you, and at some stage in your own life, you'll be extremely grateful and fulfilled with that; maybe not now, but it will happen if you're open to it.

Picking The Right Partner

The best way to avoid major compatibility problems is to pick your partners wisely. Again, you're not known for thinking before you jump, but perhaps a few minutes consideration here could you save you a major headache in the future! The best types of partners for an ESTP personality type have similar traits, but not identical. Two ESTPs may work, but there is also the chance they could butt heads and cause a serious migraine for one another. The best traits for you to look for include:

- An introvert. Yes, really! This can help ground and balance an ESTP
- Someone who has a spontaneous element to their personality
- Someone who wants a future, but doesn't feel rushed to do so in the here and now

- Someone who isn't overly emotional in their approach to life
- Someone who is driven and hardworking

That is all you really need. If you go for someone who is extroverted and wants to live in the here and now, just like you, then that union isn't going to be one which helps you grow. Going for someone who is more introverted will help balance out those wild elements of your own personality, and keep you grounded, helping you to appreciate the more homely elements of life.

8
Conclusion

And there you have it, the confusing, adventurous, fulfilling, and very active life of an ESTP. We've covered a lot of ground, and it's important that you take the time to really digest the information we've given you. It's a good idea to take each chapter apart one by one, analyze it and see if this is something which actually affects you or not.

Remember, just because you marked as an ESTP, that doesn't mean that every single trait is going to pertain to you. We are very rarely 100% of one type, and a lot of the time we are more closely matched to one type, but with a subtle mix of other types thrown in for good measure. That means that not every strength and weakness will call out to you, but most will do. So, for that reason, sit down and work out which ones you really need to focus on, and for the ones you're not sure of, perhaps have a chat with a loved one, someone who knows you really well, to find out whether that is something which affects you too. Sometimes we're a little blind to our own traits, purely because we're the ones living them!

Another point to take away is not to be disheartened by any of the weaknesses we have talked about. The main focus of this book is to celebrate the wonderful personality type that you are! The fact that you have weaknesses is a good thing, because it means you have room to develop and move without being stuck in one place. None of us are perfect, and if we were then life would be rather dull and boring. Weaknesses make us human, and that is not something you should ever try and change. The quest for perfection is a fruitless one, so the best course of action is to simply aim to minimize the effect your weaknesses have on your life, by ensuring they don't put roadblocks and limitations in your way. When you do this, you open your life up to much more opportunities, allowing you to reach potential that you didn't even realize you had.

So, sit back, relax, grab a pen and paper, and explore your wonderful ESTP world!

Note from the author

Thank you for purchasing and reading this book. If you enjoyed it or found it useful then I'd really appreciate it if you would post a short review on Amazon. I do read all the reviews personally so that I can continually write what people are wanting.

If you'd like to leave a review then please visit the link below:

https://www.amazon.com/dp/B079MDZ41F

Thanks for your support and good luck!

Check Out My Other Books

Below you'll find some of my other books that are popular on Amazon and Kindle as well. Simply search the titles listed below on Amazon. Alternatively, you can visit my author page on Amazon to see other work done by me.

ENFP: Understand and Break Free From Your Own Limitations

INFP: Understand and Break Free From Your Own Limitations

ENFJ: Understand and Break Free From Your Own Limitations

INFJ: Understand and Break Free From Your Own Limitations

ENFP: INFP: ENFJ: INFJ: Understand and Break Free From Your Own Limitations – The Diplomat Bundle Series

INTP: Understand and Break Free From Your Own Limitations

INTJ: Understand and Break Free From Your Own Limitations

ENTP: Understand and Break Free From Your Own Limitations

ENTJ: Understand and Break Free From Your Own Limitations

ESTJ: Understand and Break Free From Your Own Limitations

ISTJ: Understand and Break Free From Your Own Limitations

ISFJ: Understand and Break Free From Your Own Limitations

ESFJ: Understand and Break Free From Your Own Limitations

ISFP: Understand and Break Free From Your Own Limitations

OPTION B: F**K IT - How to Finally Take Control Of Your Life And Break Free From All Expectations. Live A Limitless, Fearless, Purpose Driven Life With Ultimate Freedom